IMAGES
of America

WEST ORANGE

IMAGES
of America

WEST ORANGE

Joseph P. Nole II

ARCADIA

Copyright © 1998 by Joseph P. Nole II.
ISBN 0-7524-1293-0

Published by Arcadia Publishing,
an imprint of Tempus Publishing, Inc.
2 Cumberland Street
Charleston, SC 29401

Printed in Great Britain.

Library of Congress Catalog Card Number: 98-86554

For all general information contact Arcadia Publishing at:
Telephone 843-853-2070
Fax 843-853-0044
E-Mail arcadia@charleston.net

For customer service and orders:
Toll-Free 1-888-313-BOOK

Visit us on the internet at http://www.arcadiaimages.com

CONTENTS

ACKNOWLEDGMENTS

I would like to express my sincere appreciation to several people. In particular, Gregory G. Marasco, public relations consultant, who assisted me at every turn and whose patience, assistance, and inspiration were invaluable in completing this book. I would also like to thank Dan Gaby, chairman of the West Orange Public Relations Commission, for assistance with reproduction of photographs; Paul Ladell, who reproduced photographs; The West Orange Public Library, for allowing me to select from its vast archives; The Newark Public Library, who provided photographs; The U.S. Department of the Interior National Park Service, Edison National Historic Site, who provided photographs and information; Joe Caltaldo of the Essex County Country Club, who provided photographs and information; the West Orange Public Relations Commission; former New Jersey Governor Brendan Byrne, who provided photographs; and township residents Leon Schneider, Judy Williams, Phyllis Ficarotta, Abe Lando, Dorothy Robertson, Bob Kraeuter, and Natalie Persson, all of whom provided photographs and information. And for their support along the way my mother, father, and sister, who continue to believe.

A MOUNTAIN VIEW

The Township of West Orange is part of the metropolitan area that surrounds Newark and New York, lying west of both cities in the center of Essex County, New Jersey. Its 12.15 square miles spread over two ridges and two valleys of the Watchung Mountains; the rolling terrain gives variety to the township and is responsible for its division into several neighborhoods.

West Orange is primarily a residential community, with approximately 40,000 citizens living in about 14,500 dwelling units, the majority of which are one-family homes. There are some manufacturing industries, but the greatest business development has been in office buildings, retail establishments, medical buildings, and personal services.

About one-fifth of the land is open space, consisting of municipal and county parks and playgrounds, private and public golf courses, and undeveloped acreage. Portions of Essex County's South Mountain and Eagle Rock Reservation contain picnic areas, hiking trails, ball fields, and bridle paths in the woods. Eagle Rock Reservation includes a lookout from which one can see the skyscrapers of New York, the Statue of Liberty, and the George Washington and Verazzano Bridges. On a clear night, the view is spectacular.

In the beginning, the first people known to have lived in West Orange were the Lenni-Lenape Indians. In fact, Lenni-Lenape means "original people." Evidence of their presence can be substantiated by the name "Wigwam Brook"—an indication that Indians once lived in the Tory Corner area—and the remains of the intersecting Indian paths at the notches at Eagle Rock, Mount Pleasant, and Northfield Avenues.

The tract of land that the Lenni-Lenape Indians owned was purchased by a group of Puritans who, led by Robert Treat and John Gregory, migrated from Connecticut in 1666. The purchase price of this land, roughly the size of Essex County, was 1 half-penny per acre, converted by mutual consent into useful goods—bars of lead, barrels of gunpowder, clothing, blankets, guns, and liquor.

The Lenni-Lenape Indian trails followed the watercourses. Swinefield Road (now Washington Street, Main Street, and Eagle Rock Avenue) was one mountain trail so named because swine were driven by this route to Livingston for summer pasture. Christian Path was another trail followed by early settlers who walked from their homes over the mountain to church in Orange. Pilgrim Cross, originally on Ridge Road near Northfield Avenue, marked the place where they stopped to put on their shoes after walking barefoot to that point to save shoe leather. The cross is now on the site of the Saint Cloud Presbyterian Church.

The Colony of Newark was the original settlement in Essex County, called "Pesayak Towne," but the hardworking, God-fearing people soon occupied land to the west. In 1678, Anthony

Olef (or Olive) arrived on the "Treat Mountain Watchung," surveyed the land, and subsequently built a farm in what is now Llewellyn Park. In 1780, the entire area west of Newark was given the name of Orange in honor of the English Royal House of Orange.

Among the earliest occupations of the residents were sheep-raising and wool-spinning, apple-growing, and the processing of cider and apple whiskey. They also produced grain, fruits, and vegetables from the rich soil with natural drainage. The region was its own Eden with beautiful trees, rivers, and springs.

Sandstone and trap-rock quarrying were important industries by 1700. The availability of water and the profusion of hemlock trees that grew on the mountain slopes developed other industries. The ready and cheap source of tanbark allowed for the manufacture of boots and shoes.

Because of the relatively rugged and mountainous character of the terrain, the territory in the western part of the county earned for itself the name of "The Mountain Society." The small hamlet in the vicinity of what are now Washington and Main Streets was known as Williamstown (later Tory Corner), and that to the south near the intersection of Valley Road and Freeman Street had the name Freemantown. Both appellations were derived from the names and political affiliations of the principal families who had originally settled in these two localities.

The mountain territory separated the relatively rich farming counties of Warren, Sussex, and Morris to the west from the growing communities to the east at the mouths of the Passaic and Hackensack Rivers and on the waters of New York Bay. Although from the standpoint of distance the natural mountain trails were the shortest links between the two sections, the steep grades encountered at the ridges acted as a barrier to travel. Furthermore, the remoteness of the territory from the growing settlement of Newark tended to offset the advantages of healthful climate, high elevation, and good drainage. The early inhabitants, consequently, had to be almost entirely self-sustaining, and farming and the home processing of farm products were the principal activities.

One hundred thirty-six years ago the County of Essex comprised the City of Newark and the Townships of Caldwell, Livingston, Millburn, Clinton, Orange, Bloomfield, and Belleville, which had been split off from the Township of Newark at various times by acts of the state legislature.

On March 11, 1862, the Township of Fairmount was created by the legislature from portions of Caldwell, Livingston, and the section of Orange west of what is now Prospect Avenue (formerly Perry Lane) on top of the First Mountain. One year later on March 14, 1863, the entire eastern slope of the First Mountain was carved out of the western part of Orange at the instigation of certain prominent citizens who were dissatisfied with the manner in which the public schools were being conducted. This territory was added to the adjoining Township of Fairmount and called the Township of West Orange. It was created from the eastern portion of the Township of Orange.

The first school in the new township, Saint Mark's, opened in 1865 near the present entrance to Llewellyn Park. Its nine classrooms accommodated 470 students. A second school was built in 1878 at Valley Road and Mitchell Street. Washington School, erected in 1895, is the oldest still in use in West Orange.

In 1884, West Orange established a police department with a chief, a captain, and three men. Ten years later, a fire department was organized with three paid men and eight men on call.

More than a decade earlier, Llewellyn S. Haskell fell in love with the beauty and invigorating air of the mountains and purchased 20 acres of land at Turke Eagle Rock, so named because of the eagles that nested there. Here he built a rustic home, The Eyrie, which was for many years a landmark in the Eagle Rock Reservation.

Next he conceived the idea of a beautiful residential park on the mountainside. He purchased nearly 800 acres of farmland and promptly began transforming them into a wooded retreat with winding roads, brooks, cascades, gardens, and sites for elegant homes. Llewellyn Park became the first residential park in the United States built according to a total plan, and it still has the natural scenic beauty and the winding roads—illuminated by gaslights—that existed more than a century ago.

Llewellyn Park Proprietors, who are the owners of the acreage, meet annually to elect a committee of managers and to set the park tax rate. Upkeep of the common land and roads, as well as police patrols, are provided for by the residents. However, they rely on the Township for fire and additional police protection.

One of the many noted people to have lived in West Orange, and in particular Llewellyn Park, was Thomas Alva Edison. Edison lived and worked in West Orange from 1886 until his death in 1931. His laboratory buildings, which he designed and constructed, were the best equipped and most efficient of the time, and they served as models for the great laboratories of the present. During his time in West Orange, Edison was granted 520 patents on such inventions as electric motors and generators, storage batteries, long-playing records, dictating machines, fluorescent lamps, and motion pictures.

Edison's home in Llewellyn Park, Glenmont, is a charming, 19th-century house. It is situated on 13 acres of beautifully landscaped grounds in Llewellyn Park and still contains the furnishings, books, mementos, and gifts from people all over the world that were accumulated when Thomas Edison lived there.

For a great many years, no change in the simple existence of the people in the mountain section was apparent, but about 1890 an evolution began to take place. The migration of industry to this region played a large role in its development. Whether because raw materials were cheaper here, because new inventions made it easier to do business, or because of labor difficulties in other areas, industry began to favor this community. In addition, the topography, drainage, and geological characteristics of the land exerted a profound effect on its growth. Most significantly, perhaps, transportation improved dramatically and made the community much more accessible.

When West Orange was formed, its roads and streets were hardly more than wagon trails, dusty in the summer and fall and muddy in winter and spring. The township committee appointed a board of road overseers at its first meeting in 1863, and funds were raised for improving Northfield Avenue. Many miles of road were built throughout the area after Daniel Brennan installed the first stone crusher in 1868; two years later Brennan imported the first steamroller from England.

One horse-drawn stage line operated between Orange and Livingston, and another from the foot of Eagle Rock to Pleasantdale in 1878. A cable road near Orange Heights Avenue was built by the Orange Mountain Cable Company in 1893. The tracks ran in a straight line from the valley to the top of the mountain; cars were pulled by cable to a point near the present clubhouse of the Rock Spring Country Club. A hotel, pond, and amusement park were built at the top of the mountain by promoters anticipating a new vacation center. The resort was known as Highland Park or Cable Lake, but unfortunately the project was not successful.

A horse car that ran from Newark to Main and Washington Streets was in operation in 1890. In 1892, the first electrical car was operating in the same section and had an extension that carried the line along Eagle Rock Avenue (now Main Street) to Harrison Avenue. The growth of Edison Industries was one of the principal reasons for the extension.

As we know, sandstone removal, cutting, and dressing provided work for the local inhabitants as early as 1700. At various times, there were as many as three quarries producing sandstone for building purposes and for headstones in the local cemeteries. The sandstone quarry in the "Ramble" in Llewellyn Park provided the stone from which Saint John's Church in Orange was constructed. Schrump's quarry on the eastern slope of the Second Mountain north of Eagle Rock Avenue was the source of the stone from which Saint Mark's Church was built. The sandstone quarries all ceased operation at the beginning of this century and practically no evidence of early activity remains.

For a great many years, it was recognized that the waters of Wigwam Brook and the East Branch of the Rahway River were of a quality suitable for the processing of men's felt hats and the tanning of leather for boots and shoes. Furthermore, the hemlock trees that grew in profusion on the mountain slopes were a ready and cheap source of tan bark. Consequently, in the early days, the manufacture of hats and shoes was carried on either by individuals or in small establishments located on these watercourses. The market for the products was limited to the immediate locality because all operations were done by hand and the business, of necessity, was conducted on a small scale.

Although the Morris & Essex line avoided the town limits, the coming of the new railroad had some compensating advantages because it contributed to the growth of Orange as an industrial center and indirectly stimulated growth in the eastern section of West Orange. About the same time that the railroad appeared, the introduction of steam revolutionized the methods of manufacturing hats and shoes and stimulated the invention of all sorts of devices to increase their production and reduce costs. Mechanical developments in the shoe industry in other sections of the country made that industry unprofitable in Orange; by 1862 there was little activity in it. The hat manufacturers, on the other hand, had kept pace with the basic new inventions patented in the 1850–1860 decade and were thus in position to capitalize upon the cheap rail transportation to Newark and New York.

The Township of West Orange has afforded its inhabitants the opportunity for growth and development. The individuals who have guided its destiny during the past three centuries were quick to recognize the natural advantages with which the territory was endowed; were untiring in their efforts to overcome the mountain barriers that held back the growth of the western section for so many years; and were instrumental in developing the material, moral, and mental life of the community. The job they started is not finished, as all communities continue to develop over time. Their work has but laid the foundation upon which the leaders of the present can build a better community in which to live and of which future generations will be proud.

One

AROUND THE TOWN

The Township of West Orange is a residential suburb of the big cities of Newark and New York. There are many neighborhoods in West Orange. Two of the most well-known and historic are Tory Corner and Llewellyn Park. Other neighborhoods include Pleasantdale, Saint Cloud, Hazel, Gregory, Redwood, and Eagle Rock.

Because of the ruggedness of the territory, the original mountain trails made by the Indians and later developed by the early settlers followed the watercourses until the slope became too difficult for easy traveling. One of these early mountain trails was the Swinefield Road (now Eagle Rock Avenue), which derived its name from the fact that the inhabitants of Williamstown drove their swine by this route to the Passaic Valley in Livingston for summer pasturage. The early roads paralleling the mountains also followed the streams because settlers found it convenient to locate their homes near reliable water supplies.

Shortly after the Township of Fairmount was incorporated, two real estate developments of note got underway. Dr. Edgar E. Marcy acquired some 200 acres of land bounded by the ridge of the First Mountain, Northfield Road, Mount Pleasant Avenue, and Prospect Avenue. Dr. Marcy cleared this heavily wooded tract and thus acquired an unobstructed view of the growing cities of Newark and New York to the east. General George B. McClellan of Civil War fame and John Crosby Brown, a prominent New York banker, were members of the colony of famous people who erected fine homes along the "ridge," or "brow," as it was sometimes called.

About the same time, Benjamin Small was promoting another real estate development just to the south. This development, which was given the name of Saint Cloud, consisted mostly of small cottages and was more of a summer colony than Dr. Marcy's development. The people who built their homes in both of these sections were of considerable means and, consequently, in the summer the town took on a lively appearance. Handsome equipages drawn by well-groomed horses and driven by coachman in livery passed up and down the mountain roads carrying the men to and from the Orange Station in the morning and evening, and taking their ladies calling during the late mornings and afternoons.

The Township of West Orange has changed but it retains the agricultural and rural complexion of its early days.

At the turn of the century, a number of streets began branching off from Main Street in the town center when the real estate boom started. Most of the streets in the town are named for company officials responsible for the township's prosperity, prominent families, local politicians, judges, war heroes, athletes, natural features, flowers, trees, states, expressions, or patriotic events.

In 1863, only three roads ran out from Main Street, and these were no more than dirt or—depending on the season—mud paths. One, Valley Road, ran through the valley, and another, Northfield Avenue (pictured here), came through the north of town. A third road, Eagle Rock Avenue, led to Eagle Rock.

In this 1920 photograph, a concerned citizen with a police escort attempts to get the word out to the voting public concerning a referendum on whether or not the township should increase taxes.

This mailman remains true to his code. The snowfall, albeit meager, does not prevent him from delivering the mail to residents of West Orange. Note the uniform, or apparent lack thereof. This photograph is from the early 1900s.

Two children, perhaps an older sister with her younger brother, take a stroll through a wooded section of West Orange during a beautiful fall day. Note that the girl is wearing a hat, which was customary in earlier times.

This typical Colonial farmhouse formerly stood near Washington Street and Franklin Avenue. Eight generations lived in this house, which was built in 1725. It was said to have been the headquarters of Gen. George Washington during the Revolutionary War. In the hallway was an old-fashioned clock, which had been brought surreptitiously from Elizabethtown to escape the exorbitant tax imposed by the British authorities. Southeast of the house stood an old sawmill.

This house belonged to John Condit, who came to America and settled in Newark c. 1678. His descendants multiplied and spread throughout the northern part of the state and elsewhere. The family has been closely identified with the political, commercial, social, and religious life of this and other nearby states. In the summer of 1905, at a Condit gathering in West Orange, it was decided to organize an association for the lineal descendants of John Condit (or Cundit).

The rich and fertile soil of the land in West Orange allowed the colonists in the area to sell their produce for a high profit at the farmers' markets in Newark and New York City. Farmers on their way to market from the western lands of Morris County rested in the community after residents developed lodging for them. The lodging business proved to be a very lucrative one.

This house belonged to Gen. George B. McLellan, affectionately known to his troops and friends as "Little Mac" and the 34th governor of New Jersey (1878–1881). Commander of the Potomac during the Civil War, he defended Washington against Robert E. Lee but was dismissed by President Abraham Lincoln as commander of the main Northern forces. McLellan failed to pursue Lee and deal the Confederates a decisive blow at the Battle of Antietam in 1862.

The Rock Mineral Spring on Northfield Avenue just opposite Walker Road is shown here in the 1920s. The discovery of the spring in 1820 launched suburban and recreational development in West Orange's Watchung Mountains. Believed to contain minerals that would cure sickness and disease, the town mineral spring was attractive to city dwellers from Newark and New York City who spent their summers here.

This image depicts the end of the West Orange car line on Eagle Rock Avenue. The first electric car of the Orange & Newark Horse Car Railway on Eagle Rock Avenue was completed in 1892. The company had lines that extended up Main Street from Lincoln Avenue in Orange to the West Orange boundary and then along Valley Road to Tory Corner.

The idea behind the construction of the Eagle Rock trolley line—pictured here—was to provide cheap transportation to Eagle Rock, which had become a mecca for Sunday picnickers because of its high elevation and magnificent view of the growing metropolitan area. In addition to the view, there was the small ice pond to the west of the ridge at the intersection of Eagle Rock and Prospect Avenues. The owners rented rowboats to the picnickers in the summertime and provided facilities for skating in the winter. As a result, the spot soon became so popular that a dance hall, restaurant, and merry-go-round were constructed. The enterprise was called Crystal Lake Amusement Park on Crystal Lake.

Car #8001, bound for Penn Station via Orange Street, picks up small contingent of war workers at the Edison plant on Lakeside Avenue. Bunting is out for the Memorial Day holiday, draped from the trolley span wires.

This photograph of the Orange line car #3253 provides an excellent view of the Tory Corner's eastside business section. This section of town prospered quickly and continues to be a staple of the community.

The war is on in earnest now and trolleys carry Red Cross posters. Car #2621 saw service on the #43 Jersey City line until that line was transitioned to all-service vehicles in 1938. It was then assigned to the Orange line.

This is the inside of a public service, single-ended "deluxe" trolley car, able to seat close to 50 people (with standees, the capacity reached 100). The buses that replaced these cars could only hold 36 passengers. The deluxe car included numerous amenities: each window was equipped with its own shade and powerful electric heaters operated under each seat so that no one would feel the cold. The grooves in the flooring carried off melting snow in the winter. Two trapdoors in the floor (seen in the immediate foreground) gave access to the trucks below, and to the two electric motors carried on each truck. In the lower right corner is the sandbox, from which sand could be chuted to the track below to enhance traction.

This photograph depicts a busy Tory Corner in the summer of 1940. Two 48-foot behemoths dominate the scene—each 22 tons of wood and steel. The automobiles seem tiny beside them. Washington School, which witnessed the transition from horse cars to electric cars in the 19th century, is obscured by the trees.

A natural, healthy country town nestled in the mountains and surrounded by pure air and all of nature's advantages and yet only 13 miles from New York City, West Orange proved to be a magnet for many sports buffs, as this photograph taken in 1900 illustrates.

This photograph was taken on July 2, 1900. It depicts four men enjoying the winter snow with a toboggan slide on Hazel Avenue. This annual event was sponsored by the Essex County Toboggan Club.

Children at play take a break from their football game to have their picture taken. Note the football, which is much larger in the middle than the footballs of today. Not surprisingly, the fatter football made it difficult to grip the ball and throw it. It is no wonder that the concept of the forward pass developed later in the century.

The South Mountain Arena in West Orange is home to the Turtle Back Zoo and serves as a practice venue for the former world-champion New Jersey Devils hockey team. The Devils practice at the ice rink inside almost every day during the hockey season. The rink and zoo are open to the public.

Two

EAGLE ROCK AND CRYSTAL LAKE

West Orange has many attractive sights, and two in particular deserve to be examined closely. Eagle Rock Reservation offers a commanding view of the township and Crystal Lake contributes to a significant part of the township's rich history.

Eagle Rock is a bold rock ledge of 664 feet. The panoramic view from this elevation stretches east from the Passaic-Hackensack Valleys to Newark and New York. Eagle Rock was used by Washington as one in a chain of observation posts extending from Patterson to Summit. From here, the countryside below was scanned for Tory raiders.

Eagle Rock was so named because eagles nested among the crags and rocks. Llewellyn Haskel, founder of Llewellyn Park, made the first purchase of Eagle Rock land in 1853. In 1854, he started building Eyrie, his home, a unique castellated structure that was for many years a landmark of Eagle Rock Reservation.

In 1894, a trolley line was put into operation from Orange to Cox's Hotel on Mountain Avenue at the foot of Eagle Rock. The Essex County Park Commission purchased 408 acres in 1895 and established the Eagle Rock Reservation. The reservation became a very popular mecca for Sunday picnickers during the late 19th century because of its magnificent view of the New Jersey, New York, and Staten Island skylines.

Crystal Lake also served as a terrific gathering place for families on a typical summer day. The children could play on the merry-go-round and other rides and families could fish, swim, picnic, or go boating. The main attraction of the lake was "The Grove," a delightful green pasture cherished by all lake-goers. Several community activists, such as Thomas A. Edison and former Commissioner George V. McDonough, as well as many civic groups, clubs, business groups, and political organizations, organized and sponsored picnics and outings at Crystal Lake.

A day at the lake usually peaked in the afternoon, when some form of entertainment was put into place. This usually involved the creation of a makeshift boxing ring, in which the various boxing clubs—so prevalent in the Hudson and Essex County areas—would show off their new club fighters. Tony Galento, famous for almost deposing Joe Louis, the premiere fighter of his day, was a participant in a few Sunday-afternoon fights.

Eagle Rock and Crystal Lake are two of the extremely rare vehicles that forge connections between local history and modern life. We know that their pleasures will be enjoyed by the generations of tomorrow as well.

A look through the opening of Eagle Rock Reservation offers a commanding view at an elevation of 664 feet. It is reported that this view includes a greater concentration of suburban dwellings than any other in the world.

During the Revolutionary War, Washington's soldiers used this as an observation post. It is the only spot in the world where one can see approximately 16 million people in just one glance.

In 1854, Llewellyn S. Haskell commenced building the Eyrie of Eagle Rock Reservation, using a plain farmhouse as the original foundation for this unique and castellated structure. The Eyrie remained in Haskell's possession until 1871 and for many years was a landmark in the Eagle Rock Reservation.

The most striking topographical feature of the reservation is the crest of Orange Mountain, the top of an enormous trap dike similar to the Palisades on the west bank of the Hudson River. Cliffs and precipitous slopes form the eastern face of the mountain. The crest is from 597 to 664 feet above sea level; it is over 300 feet above the valley and gentling rolling country that begins only about a quarter of a mile to the east. The eastern boundary of the reservation runs approximately along the contour of the mountain about 100 feet below the crest.

The trolley line to the foot of Eagle Rock was placed in operation in 1894. The idea behind the construction of the Eagle Rock line was to provide cheap transportation to Eagle Rock. The promoters of the line realized the impracticability of running a trolley to the top of the ridge because of the excessive grades. Instead, they counted upon their patrons climbing the last 100 feet up a zigzag path constructed along the side of the cliff, which rises precipitously at that point. The trolley venture was not a financial success at first and after a few years the Crosstown and Eagle Rock lines went into receivership.

At this point a traveler could walk up the famous one hundred steps to the top of Eagle Rock. In 1894 an extension of the Washington Street Trolley line went to the foot of Eagle Rock.

On summer holidays and Sunday mornings, a steady stream of trolley cars left Newark via the Orange line for the terminus at Harrison Avenue, where passengers either walked up the mountain to the top—like the people pictured here—or transferred to the Eagle Rock line. In the late afternoon and evening the homeward trek began and the streak of trolley cars on the Orange line reversed itself, carrying the tired but happy trippers back to their hot homes.

Residents take in the glorious view that is offered by Eagle Rock Reservation. On certain days, the open cars on both the Orange and Eagle Rock lines were so crowded with passengers standing inside and clinging to the running boards on both sides that conductors had to be acrobats in order to travel from one end of the car to the other collecting fares. They had to be optimists if they expected to get them all.

The Casino at Eagle Rock, on the top of Orange Mountain, provided nighttime activities for people after the accessibility of the mountain was improved with the invention of the automobile.

In 1887, the Orange Mountain Land Company was incorporated to acquire land on the mountaintop from Northfield Avenue to Walker Road. A hotel was built to attract visitors, but the original idea of real-estate development was not successful; the land company went into receivership in 1895 and 1896.

Eagle Rock Reservation occupies the northeast corner of West Orange and a small strip of Montclair. Directly east of it lies the southern part of Montclair, and, further east, the northern part of Bloomfield. Llewellyn Park touches the southern extremity of Eagle Rock, and Verona lies north of it. Massive boulders and great forest trees give a rugged appearance and add much to the environment of the reservation.

The Eagle Rock Reservation ice cream pavilion must have been a welcome sight on summer days. Many flocked to the pavilion to get ice cream after picnicking with family and friends on "The Grove."

While waiting for the trolley to take them back to their homes after a relaxing day of picnicking and playing various games, the day-trippers could wait in this shelter out of the hot summer sun.

Thinking back to the days of the Revolutionary War, we can easily imagine these mountaineers as soldiers looking out for incoming ships. Note the horse-drawn buggy in the left of the photograph; it offered visitors an opportunity to sit back and enjoy their day in style.

West Orange is very fortunate to possess such a large number of parks, both public and private. Eagle Rock, preserved forever in its pristine state under the Essex County Park Commission, is visited annually by throngs of people who seek out this world-renowned natural wonder.

A visitor to Eagle Rock Reservation takes a look at what remains of the bridge that went over the cable road at the crest of the First Mountain in West Orange. Lack of use and years of decay have caused the bridge to look like this.

This photograph captures the view over West Orange as seen through the gorge used for cable-car travel to Crystal Lake. Steel framework is all that is left of the bridge today.

Boating and fishing were popular activities for visitors to Crystal Lake, which was located in Eagle Rock Park on the top of Orange Mountain. Fishing was also prevalent. Nine species were known to live in the lake, including goldfish and wide-mouthed bass.

Crystal Lake, 4.5 acres in area, was a spring-fed lake. This meant that no one could alter it or fill it in. The cooling effect of the springs could make the water temperature range from 4 to 7 degrees cooler than it otherwise would have been.

Both rowboats and canoes were offered at the lake. The canoe was the more stylish of the two boats and its operation required more skill. It was more enjoyable, yet was more vulnerable. The canoe was usually limited to two passengers.

The rear paddleman in the canoe, in tandem with the front paddleman, could maneuver a quick, 90-degree or 180-degree turn. However, persons who tried to stand up and change seats in a canoe often found themselves immersed in 4 to 5 feet of water.

There wasn't much activity during the winter months, yet the cold gray skies still brought tourists to the frozen lake to enjoy a relaxing diversion and community camaraderie, particularly on the weekends.

CRYSTAL LAKE TOP OF ORANGE MOUNTAIN

When it came time to eat after a day's activities at the lake, the fare was hearty and traditional. There were roast beef sandwiches—succulent and juicy—served at a four-sided frame stand. Gleaming yellow and white corn in large, steaming, coal-fed metal vats was available at another four-sided stand. Raw clams on the half-shell were served and were popular. Burly, no-nonsense bartenders with garters around their upper arms served up brew from the wooden barrel kegs; other kegs were kept standing by, just waiting to be tapped. Even with all of the lively music and activity, one could still hear the sounds of the steel horseshoe hitting the metal pegs in the background.

Three

THE ENCHANTED
GROUND

The little rustic lodge that guards the Llewellyn Park entrance looks somewhat out of place at the busy intersection of Main Street and Park Avenue. If it were not for the rich history that surrounds Llewellyn Park, most passersby would not realize what it is—420 acres and 17 miles of "the first romantic suburb," a paradise and "an enchanted ground."

It has been said that there was nothing visionary about the park's planning and incorporation. Llewellyn S. Haskell's architect friend, Alexander Jackson Davis, sold him on the idea of a "retreat for business men and intellectuals" on the slopes of Orange Mountain below Eagle Rock.

Founded in 1857, Llewellyn Park became the first residential park in the United States. The slogan used to promote the dwellings in this community was "Country Homes for City People." Four years before the park's founding, Haskell fell in love with the beauty and invigorating air of the mountains and purchased 20 acres of land at Turke Eagle Rock, so named because of the eagles that nested there. It is at this spot that Haskell supervised construction of a Tennysonian tower called the Eyrie; it stood a decaying monument until it was torn down in 1924.

As one moves along the curved roads, the grassy borders, and shrubbery, it would seem that he is miles away from a city. Such was Mr. Haskell's intention when he engaged Frederick Law Olmstead, one of the designers of the then-sensational Central Park, to lay the roads out in their meandering pattern.

As one continues along the roads, he comes upon Glenmont, the world-famous home of Mr. and Mrs. Thomas A. Edison. The great red house towers amid acres of green lawns.

Another landmark is Castlewood, perched high on the Orange Mountain slope. Dominated by two massive towers and complete with dungeon, it is set on the hill in two levels. Several early owners went broke trying to finish Castlewood's 2-foot-thick stone walls and medieval tower, from which one can see the George Washington Bridge.

Llewellyn Park has undergone many changes over the past one hundred years. Many of the big old estates, with such flowery names as Blytheles, Bonnair, and Baronald, have been whittled down or broken up and their rambling mansions torn down or remodeled. However, Llewellyn Park still has the natural scenic beauty and the winding roads—illuminated by gaslights—that existed more than a century ago.

This is a statue of Llewellyn Park founder, Llewellyn S. Haskell, born in 1815. Haskell was a successful drug importer who loved natural scenery, mountains, and forests. An avid supporter of plans to construct Central Park in New York City, he lived on an estate on the Passaic River until the death of one of his sons in 1852. The following year he visited the southwestern slope of Orange Mountain (now West Orange) and saw streams and picturesque ravines as well as the potential for a beautiful garden in the area's dense woods.

Many changes have altered the look of the park over the past one hundred years, but the rustic lodge where the park policeman stands has been there from the start. The official prevents troublemakers from slipping through the iron gates.

All of Llewellyn Park's roads are shaded by trees; thousands of exotic flowers; bushes; rare plant life imported from Europe, South America, and Asia; stone bridges; and the overall solemn stillness of the area. Road-planning was another of Llewellyn Haskell's hobbies. He later pioneered the creation of the Essex County Road Board, the forerunner of the highways and bridges committee.

Llewellyn Park Proprietors, who are the owners of the acreage, meet annually to elect a committee of managers and to set the park tax rate. Residents provide for the upkeep of the common land and roads and for their police patrols, but rely on the Township for fire and additional police protection.

The Terrace Gardens, bought by Orson D. Munn, founder of *The Scientific American*, are terraced straight up the side of Orange Mountain.

Historians generally credit Llewellyn Haskell with masterminding the landscaping of Llewellyn Park, but architect Alexander Jackson Davis has been cited for creating much of the park's early architecture and developing its romantic flavor. His contributions include the gate lodge, a lyceum, and designs for several homes.

Glenmont, the charming, 19th-century home of the late Mr. and Mrs. Thomas A. Edison, is situated on 13 acres of beautifully landscaped grounds in Llewellyn Park. It still contains the furnishings, books, mementos, and gifts from people all over the world that were accumulated when Thomas Edison lived there. The buildings and grounds have recently undergone major refurbishing.

Llewellyn Park became the first residential park in the United States built according to a total plan, and it still has the natural scenic beauty and the winding roads that existed more than a century ago. However, due to various encroachments, the park is only a little more than half its original size.

We're off for a drive along curving roads; the grassy borders and shrubbery along the side are kept up by the residents. When Llewellyn Haskell engaged Frederick Law Olmstead to lay out the roads, he instructed him to do it without incorporating a straight line from one end to the other.

The basic design of Llewellyn Park was set in 1857. The land contour consisted of a mile-long slope marked by rows of natural terraces. The slope was cut diagonally by the erratic course of a plunging mountain brook, whose deep ravines were the main feature of the 50-acre park. Villa sites, reached by winding roads, were set on brook borders and terraces.

Llewellyn Park has undergone many changes since its beginning. Yet, Willow Brook still surges through the ramble's ravines, park roads wind through spacious forests, and enough representations of the early architecture remain to give an observer the flavor of America's first romantically landscaped park.

Llewellyn Haskell supervised construction of the Eyrie, a Tennysonian tower, near what is now Eagle Rock Avenue. Haskell covered its outer walls with bark with his own hands. It stood a decaying monument until it was torn down in 1924.

The rich and famous of Llewellyn Park still liked a morning paper; here a paperboy does the rounds, bringing papers to the Edison mansion, to the home of Charles Edison (later governor), and to dozens of other affluent customers.

The Llewellyn Park residence of Mr. Edgar S. Bamberger was designed by Clifford C. Wendehack. Most of the homes in Llewellyn Park were the first important purchases of land by the park proper in the community's development.

This Victorian style home was designed by Alexander Jackson Davis in 1855. Davis sold Haskell on the idea of "a retreat for business men and intellectuals" on the slopes of Orange Mountain below Eagle Rock.

Castlewood was another famous Llewellyn Park landmark. Its stone walls are 2 feet thick and the view from the medieval tower takes in the George Washington Bridge.

These are the boys of the Carteret School Summer Day Camp. Together with Director Ed Rochford, they enjoy a swim on the former estate of the late Everett Colby in 1949. The perpetuation of Llewellyn Park as an exclusive residential section is assured by a covenant written in every deed whereby each property owner is restricted to certain rules.

Another beautifully landscaped Llewellyn Park residence is shown here. While the park belongs to the people who live in it, the man who founded and controlled it insisted that it should be open, under proper restrictions, to the public at all times except Sundays. Unfortunately, this is no longer the case.

Four

MAN OF THE MILLENNIUM

Over its history, the Township of West Orange has been home to many noted persons. The most famous of them is Thomas Edison, world-renowned as the inventor of the phonograph, incandescent lighting, and motion pictures.

Although Edison was not born in West Orange, his fame reached its height while he was living and working here until his death in 1931. During his lifetime he received 1,093 U.S. patents—more than any other American—and numerous foreign patents.

Edison set the model for invention; before him it was at best a haphazard process. He did begin by tinkering, but once his talent became apparent he began to invent full-time. He saw his laboratories, which were the best equipped and most efficient of the time and would later become models of industrial research and development, as places devoted to the "rapid and cheaper development of inventions." Edison, who felt that no problem was unsolvable, used inspired guesses and patience along with important contributions from scientists and technicians to help him perfect his astonishing inventions.

"It is a great deal too nice for me, but it isn't half as nice for my little wife here," Edison said of his lavish home, known as Glenmont, located in the Llewellyn Park section of West Orange. He bought Glenmont as a wedding gift for his second wife, Mina. The two were married on February 24, 1886. Mina, who called herself the "home executive," would make several changes to the house over the years, including the expansion of certain rooms and the painting of the house numerous times, finally settling on a shade of red.

The Edisons entertained many guests at Glenmont, including the King of Siam, President Herbert Hoover, Helen Keller, Orville Wright, Henry Ford, Harvey Firestone, and John Burroughs.

The couple also had three children. Madeline was born in 1888, Charles in 1890, and Theodore in 1898. All three children grew up with an interest in public affairs. Madeline directed the Edison Birthplace Association in Milan, Ohio. Charles was selected by President Franklin Roosevelt as assistant secretary of the Navy and was later elected governor of New Jersey in 1940. Theodore worked with social and environmental causes. He maintained an office in West Orange until his death in 1992.

Edison died in the master bedroom at Glenmont on October 18, 1931. Originally buried in Rosedale Cemetery in Orange, Thomas and Mina were buried on the estate at the request of their children in 1963.

Edison enjoys a very rare moment to himself reading a book on the lawn at Glenmont, purchased by Edison a month before he married his second wife. Mrs. Edison chose to live in West Orange instead of in a New York City townhouse because she knew her husband preferred the country and she thought she might never see him if they lived in a bustling metropolis.

Thomas Edison's West Orange laboratory was a prototype for today's industrial research and development laboratory. Here Edison worked from 1887 until his death in 1931.

Thomas Edison boasted that his two laboratory machine shops could build anything from a lady's watch to a locomotive. In this picture the heavy machine shop is preserved as it appeared during Edison's lifetime.

At least until the end of World War II, Edison Industries used electric-powered trucks for short-range, limited duty in and near the plant in West Orange. This truck was used primarily for towing railroad boxcars in and around tight clearances outside the main plant. Note the solid rubber tires and the railcar coupling device attached to the rear. Painted leaf-green, the trucks were virtually silent in operation.

The Thomas A. Edison Laboratory was the first building built by Edison in West Orange. It is located at the corner of Lakeside Avenue and Main Street. Some of Edison's lesser-known but significant inventions, some of which were developed in this building, include several improvements to the telegraph and telephone, the first practical fluoroscope, improvements in ore-milling and cement-making technology, and the development of the nickel-iron-alkaline storage battery.

The liveliest room in the Edison household was the second-floor living room, where the family usually spent Sundays together. Edison would often seat himself in an armchair near the fireplace and become absorbed in study while the children played or read. They were allowed to be as noisy as they wanted because it did not distract their deaf father.

Edison is at work in an experimental room on the second-floor main laboratory. The main laboratory in West Orange was three stories high and 50 feet long. It had machine shops, an engine room, glass-blowing and pumping rooms, chemical and photographic departments, rooms for electrical testing, stockrooms, and a library.

Edison, seated at his desk in his library, swiveled to face the camera. Most of the books in Edison's library, which contained ten thousand volumes, concerned patent law.

Herbert Hoover and Edison are at the entrance to the main laboratory. Edison joked that his labs were filled with "everything from an elephant's hide to the eyeballs of a United States Senator," as well as the latest machinery and finest instruments.

Edison rides in a Bailey Electric, powered by Edison storage batteries. In the background are the main laboratory and the metallurgical laboratory. At times Edison employed as many as 20 workers in the lab. The staff included scientists and engineers with training in chemistry, physics, and mathematics.

When the Edisons purchased Glenmont, the grounds included a barn and stables, greenhouses, and a pump house. In 1908, the Edisons replaced the old barn and stables with a two-story cement garage. They also replaced the greenhouse and installed a gardener's cottage, also made of cement.

Edison's chemical lab was the prototype of the modern industrial research lab. A legend in his time, Edison received many awards including the Congressional Medal of Honor in 1928 and honorary member status in the Academy of Motion Picture Arts and Sciences in 1929.

Glenmont's dining room was built for entertaining up to 750 guests. In this room the children would often eat a light meal while Mrs. Edison read to them from the Old Testament or Shakespeare.

The large library of Glenmont served as Edison's "thought bench"—the starting point for many ideas which later took shape at his "work bench," the laboratory in the valley below.

Edison and his "little wife" Mina are at the entrance to the main laboratory building on Edison's 75th birthday. Mina—Edison's second wife—and Edison were introduced by mutual friends in 1885. They were married on February 24, 1886, in Mina's hometown of Akron, Ohio. Both husband and wife loved music and, despite his deafness, Edison enjoyed playing a pipe organ.

From left to right are Harvey Firestone, President Calvin Coolidge, Henry Ford, Edison, Russell Firestone, Mrs. Coolidge, and Col. John Coolidge. Many distinguished guests visited Glenmont during Edison's years in West Orange.

Thomas A. Edison appears with his family. From left to right are Madeline, Mina, Theodore, Charles, and Thomas. The Edison children attended boarding schools and spent their summers in West Orange at Glenmont. Each would later go on to become successful in various fields of public service.

This is the earliest known photograph of the "Black Maria," the world's first building constructed especially as a motion picture studio. Early movies, including *The Great Train Robbery*—the first full-length feature film—were made there and in nearby wooded areas. The "Black Maria" was built in 1893 and demolished in 1903.

Thomas Edison sits at his desk in the library of his West Orange laboratory using an Edison Telescribe to record a telephone conversation. The Telescribe was one of Edison's successful inventions. Some of Edison's less successful inventions included concrete furniture and his $1-million venture to separate iron ore from rock using magnets and giant conveyor belts. Technologically speaking the process worked, but richer iron ore discovered in Minnesota made the procedure unnecessary.

Edison, a tireless worker, spent many late nights in his West Orange laboratory working on his inventions. Mina made the decision to put a cot in the library of his office so that Edison wouldn't have to sleep at his desk.

59

The entrance hall, complete with rich oak grain, suggests that warmth and elegance were important parts of the Edison household. Prominent in many rooms are portraits of the Edisons and their children. Note the picture of Edison in the top left of this photograph.

All three of the Edisons' children were born in Thomas and Mina's bedroom. Today, an infant's cradle from Paris still stands in the room. It was in this room that Edison murmured his last words before dying on January 18, 1931: "It is very beautiful over there."

Edison appears with a cylinder phonograph. In 1997, Edison, the man who electrified the modern world, was selected by *Life* magazine as the most important figure of the millennium. The magazine's editors selected Edison because of his contributions to the entire world, including the revolutionary cylinder phonograph.

The Edison children play on the lawn at Glenmont, which comprises 15.5 acres of landscaped grounds and has 23 rooms, a greenhouse, and a six-car garage. The estate, originally custom built for a New York executive, was decorated in the Victorian style with gables, carved balconies, and stained-glass windows. Edison acquired the property after the original owner gave it up because of financial problems.

Thomas and Mina Edison are in the den slicing birthday cake; electric candles supply the light. Edison's achievements in the area of electricity lie in the perfection of the lamp. The lighting devices of the time were dangerous, gave off noxious fumes, and were extremely expensive to operate. Edison developed a system of current distribution that made the lamp commercially feasible and provided electricity for heat and power.

Edison appears with William G. (Billy) Bee, vice president and sales manager of the Edison Storage Battery Company, in a Detroit Electric automobile. While in his teens, Edison risked his life to save a station agent's son from being crushed by a moving train car. Due to the rescue, Edison suffered an illness that caused him to become almost totally deaf.

Edison and Francis Arthur Jones (reporter and Edison biographer) conferred in the chemistry laboratory. According to one of Edison's many biographers, Matthew Josephson, Edison worked in an intimate, intense atmosphere with a small group of workers, many of whom demonstrated a fierce loyalty to their employer. This group sometimes worked to the extreme of human endurance. Relating the story of how Edison perfected a stock printer, Josephson wrote that Edison had received a rush order for an improved model in the early 1870s. At the last moment, however, the device developed problems. The inventor gathered several of his top assistants at the plant and told them, "I've locked the door and you will stay here until the job is complete." After 60 sleepless hours, the workers had the invention running smoothly.

This photograph of Wild Bill Claire was taken in 1918. Claire was an actor who was closely affiliated with Edison. He also was a member of the first graduating class at West Orange's Thomas A. Edison Junior High School.

The desk in the left background was Edison's "thought bench" in the upstairs library of his home. It has been said of Edison that his real genius lay in the fact that he could take some impractical device and make it not only work, but work well.

The conservatory at Glenmont offers peaceful relaxation amid potted plants and gleaming sunlight. After Edison purchased Glenmont, his wife added flowers and plants to the residence which the gardening staff tended for the estate.

This is the den at Edison's mansion in Glenmont. Mina sold the estate to Thomas A. Edison, Inc. in 1946, under the condition that "Glenmont and its contents be preserved as a memorial to my dear husband and his work."

Edison's laboratory buildings and Glenmont were given to the United States by the Edison family and the McGraw Edison Company. In 1962 they were combined into the Edison National Historic Site, which is administered by the National Park Service under the U.S. Department of the Interior. Among many exhibits are Edison's desk, undisturbed since his death, his laboratories, library, many of the original models of his inventions, and a replica of the "Black Maria," the first movie studio. The archival and other collections housed at the site represent the most comprehensive source of Edison material anywhere.

Five

A HISTORY OF TRADITION

In December of 1868, Major Benjamin H. Hutton, a wealthy merchant from New York City, bought 86 acres of property in West Orange. This purchase included a country home and the estate of Hutton Park, which he would occupy with his sister, the Countess Moltke Holtfield, for many years. Major Hutton passed away while he was overseas and his heirs leased the property, including the old country home, Mansion Rome, to the founding members of the Essex County Country Club (ECCC) on December 19, 1887.

After the ECCC acquired the Hutton property and converted it into a clubhouse, the first board of governors and 57 charter members decided to hold a grand opening of the new facilities on January 2, 1888. A luncheon for five hundred people was served and the splendid affair was given extensive coverage by metropolitan newspapers of that era.

On July 20, 1889, the board of governors exercised its option to purchase the Hutton property, which lay between what is now Hutton Avenue and Linsley Avenue. The ECCC purchase included 28 acres of land, the main clubhouse, stables, greenhouses, an artificial lake, a toboggan slide, and the entire length of the ravine up to Gregory Avenue—all for $65,000.

In 1895, golf finally came to the ECCC. At a meeting of the board of directors in March of that year, a golf committee was appointed. Two months later, the committee reported that work on the course had begun. In 1918, the club bought 1.8 acres at the top of the First Mountain. Charles Banks, a noted golf architect of his time, was commissioned and produced one of the most beautiful—and difficult—courses in the state.

In 1928, the club sold off 94 acres of its Hutton Park property and bought another 161 acres, extending its holdings up Pleasant Valley Way. The west course was opened to the public in 1939 and it is regarded as one of the best such courses in the state. Over the years, ECCC members have included individuals prominent in the business and social affairs of the New York metropolitan area.

Starting with its initial layout on the eastern slope of the First Mountain, the ECCC course qualifies as one of the oldest golf clubs in the United States. It may not be *the* oldest, but surely no other country club can claim to have a past so full of tradition and wonderful memories.

This is a picture of the original Essex County Country Club in the 1890s. The ECCC was formally organized by members of the Essex County Hunt Club as a means of providing an enhanced social life and a broader range of outdoor sports for their family and friends.

Two men stand outside the entrance to Hutton Park, the original site of the club off Northfield Avenue, in 1902. In the early days of the club, it was not golf that occupied the club members. For the most part, their outdoor sports revolved around horses—riding, polo, fox hunting, or tally-ho driving. In winter there was the long slide that the Toboggan Club had set up above Valley Street.

The original club building dates from 1820, when it was erected as a hotel called the Mansion House. It was located by a wooded ravine in what later become known as Hutton Park. Vacationers and holiday seekers came over from New York mainly to enjoy the lovely surroundings, like the beautiful pond pictured here.

The club is depicted here in the 1940s. Although the appearance of this structure is most attractive, its dining room and locker facilities were considerably more limited than those of the Hutton Park clubhouse. What is now the lounge, for example, was the first dining room. The bar adjoined the dining room and faced toward the tenth fairway. Behind the bar was the kitchen in what now is the bar/grill room.

ESSEX COUNTY COUNTRY CLUB IN HUTTON PARK, WEST ORANGE, N. J.   012

In June 1950, the board of governors noted that although the golf course was among the finest in the state, "the clubhouse was sadly in need of additional modern facilities for the comfort of the members." Thereupon, the board announced it had approved a building program to convert what then was the dining room to a lounge, and build a new dining room and grill on the main floor. The locker room also was to be extended westward to accommodate 50 new lockers.

Thomas Edison, whose car is pictured here, was among the distinguished members of the club. The first officers of the club were Henry A. Page of Montrose (president), A. Pennington Whitehead of Newark (vice president), Robert Sedgwick of New York (secretary), and W. Emlen Roosevelt of Elizabeth (a cousin of President Theodore Roosevelt, treasurer). On the ECCC membership rolls of other years were the names of Edward D. Duffield (president of the Prudential Insurance Company), Lenor F. Loree (president of the Delaware and Hudson Railroad), Arthur G. Hoffman (vice president of the Great Atlantic & Pacific Tea Company), Hendon Chubb (president of Chubb & Sons), Russell and Austin Colgate (of Colgate Palmolive), George W. Merck (president of the Merck Chemical Co.), Charles M. Edison (former governor and secretary of the Navy), and Senator Joseph Frelinghuysen.

A newspaper of the time spoke of the clubhouse as being "comfortably and indeed luxuriously furnished with the lower floor arranged as parlors, reception, dining, billiard and smoking rooms. It has all the appointments of a first-class social club and will be frequented summer and winter by driving parties while receptions will be given at frequent intervals." This is quoted from an advertisement for a *March Two Step* in 1895.

Six

STAPLES OF THE COMMUNITY

Two elements that measure the strength of a community are its abilities to meet the educational and religious needs of its residents. West Orange has traditionally been proficient in both aspects of community life.

Until 1865, educational facilities in West Orange were limited to a few small private schools. In that year, the new township erected Saint Mark's School on Valley Road at a cost of $12,000. Prior to 1890, no training was provided beyond the grammar school, the few high school pupils being obliged to go to Orange to complete their education. The first high school class to be graduated from a West Orange school did so in 1893 from old Saint Mark's; nine pupils were in the graduating class.

The schools were managed by a board of school trustees prior to 1890. The newly enacted school law of that year provided for a board of education consisting of 8 elected members. In 1900, the change in the local form of government from a township to a town resulted in an increase in the size of the school board to 12 elected members. In 1913, a state law provided for board members' appointment by the mayor, rather than their election. At the same time, the membership, which had been reduced to 9, was cut to 5, at which number it has remained ever since. The expansion of the school system under the supervision of the various boards of education has kept pace with the growth of the town and with general popular demand for better educational facilities.

The spiritual needs of the territory were supplied entirely by churches in Newark and in Orange until 1827, when Saint Mark's Episcopal Church was erected at what later became the town center. Fifty years later, in 1877, the Saint Cloud Presbyterian Church had the honor of being the first church of that denomination to be organized within the present town limits. The first Methodist church was started on the Heights in 1898.

Until 1914, Saint John's Church in Orange had taken care of the large number of individuals of the Roman Catholic faith who resided in West Orange. At that time, however, Our Lady of Lourdes was established as a separate parish. Many of the residents of West Orange still maintain their connection with churches in Orange. All of the local churches and their sponsored organizations take a keen interest in local affairs and are influential in community matters.

In 1729, the first schoolhouse in the Oranges was built within the triangle formed by the intersection of Springfield Road and Valley Road. It was a framed building, 20 feet by 30 feet with 8-foot posts. The schoolhouse was roofed with shingles, sided with boards, and sealed with boards on the inside. Although there were windows on three sides, the schoolhouse had poor ventilation and lighting. It was often cold and damp in winter and extremely hot in the summer.

The Washington Street School was located at the site of the present Washington School. In the early days of education in West Orange, hornbooks were used to teach the alphabet both at home and in the grammar schools. Geography was not taught until after the Revolution. Very little English grammar was taught.

This is the Saint Cloud Elementary School. Before 1890 West Orange did not have a high school so the West Orange high school students used Orange High. In 1898, a new high school was built on Gaston Street. The high school remained there until the present site on Northfield Avenue was occupied in 1924.

Schoolchildren gather in the West Orange library. The opportunity for learning was not entirely reserved for those who could afford it. In the early spring of 1791, the *New Jersey Journal* noted that "two young Indians of the Oneida tribe lately arrived at the Orange Dale Academy."

This late 1920s picture depicts a high school graduating class. In 1890 a new law changed the administration of education in West Orange and provided for a board of education consisting of eight elected members to supersede the old system of five trustees. Public education in West Orange did not yet go beyond the grammar school; the few high school students went to Orange to complete their education.

The Saint Cloud Education Center routinely was the location for banquets honoring outstanding students and teachers. This particular banquet was held for Washington's Birthday in the 1920s. The school system continues to be a point of pride for the township residents.

Roosevelt Middle School is one of three middle schools in West Orange. Roosevelt was opened in 1932 to accommodate the rapid growth of the township's population and its need for quality education.

Before the legislative acts of 1868 and 1871, Orange lacked systematic public instruction of school-age children. Before then, public schools were funded by a combination of property taxes and tuition. Gregory School, pictured here, was opened after the legislation was well into effect in 1913.

The annual cost of educating a child in 1912 was about $50 per year. Five years later, Eagle Rock Elementary School (pictured here) opened its doors. During World War I, the increase in the cost of living coupled with the public's recognition that teacher salaries were exceptionally low brought about substantial increases in the average scale of payment. The cost of educating a child doubled.

After the 1904 completion of the Hazel Avenue Elementary School, pictured here, the old Valley School was abandoned. The original Valley School building was constructed of trap rock and consisted of several classrooms on the first floor and a hall on the second floor which was known as Llewellyn Hall.

One of the three West Orange junior high schools is shown here. Prior to 1890, the schools were managed by a board of school trustees. The newly enacted school law of that year provided for a board of education consisting of 8 elected members. In 1900, the change in the local form of government from a township to a town resulted in an increase in the size of the school board to 12 elected members.

Recreation has always been an important facet of a well-rounded education. Pictured here is the 1927 West Orange Junior High School basketball team. This photograph was taken on the steps outside the school. Children in the educational system are offered a wide variety of extracurricular activities, from reading clubs to basketball.

The Pleasantdale School, pictured here, was erected in 1870 on Eagle Rock Road in the valley beyond Eagle Rock. The Valley School, a frame structure, was built in 1878 at Valley Road and Hazel Avenue at a cost of $10,000 and was used until 1904 when the Hazel Avenue School was built.

Saint Cloud School was on Swamp Road between the First and Second Mountains near Northfield Road. It dates back to 1886.

A photograph of a home economics classroom illustrates the complete education that West Orange children receive. Graduates of West Orange schools have traditionally been well-grounded in the fundamentals of life skills as well as in secondary education. Since the inception of education in West Orange, graduates have been able to hold their own in college and in business against the graduates of other high and preparatory schools across the country.

Built in 1927, Edison Junior High School was, of course, named in honor of West Orange's favorite son, Thomas Alva Edison. In today's day and age its seems that one cannot walk into a room, turn on a light switch, and not think about Edison.

Before 1827 the residents of West Orange had to depend on other towns to fulfill their spiritual needs. The Masonic Temple in Orange was among the parishes that West Orange residents utilized until the rapid growth of churches in West Orange took place, beginning with Saint Mark's in 1827.

St. Marks Church
West Orange, N. J.

Saint Mark's was first founded as a mission church in 1808 and a building was erected on the present Main Street site in 1837. Its present form took shape in 1860 when Richard Upjohn, an architect famous for his Gothic Revival churches, planned and designed a substantial addition to the older building. This picture was taken around 1900.

Rev. Paul T. Carew, former rector of Saint John's Church in Orange is at the left; Rev. Nichols A. Marnell, former rector of the new parish, is in the center; and Rev. Francis M. Reilly, assistant to Father Carew, is at the right. The clergy are gathered at the groundbreaking ceremonies for Our Lady of Lourdes Church in 1926. Today, the church building houses both a church and a full-time school.

The history of West Orange was largely shaped by the values of the churches in the town. Legislative matters in the West Essex region were brought before the local church leaders and family social life centered around Sunday services.

Church members did most of the work on the Pleasantdale Presbyterian Church, pictured here, but they also had some help from many local, non-member residents. During the early years of the church, growth was slow but steady. Church and Sunday school sessions were conducted in German. Evening services in English began on the last Sunday of November in 1888 for the benefit of English-speaking friends and neighbors.

This is the interior of Saint Mark's Church. Saint Mark's was originally part of Trinity Church in Newark, the oldest Episcopal church in Essex County (it boasted a 1746 charter from King George II). Saint Mark's was established when an act of the New Jersey state legislature separated the two parishes.

From its first service in June 1877, the Saint Cloud Presbyterian Church's members have made it a true, family-oriented congregation serving not only its own people, but those of the community and many missions wherever and whenever needs are found.

Plays are still a staple of church and school entertainment today. This photograph depicts actors in full costume during a break in a church-sponsored performance of a play in the early 1900s.

Seven

SERVING THE COMMUNITY

Fairmount and West Orange operated under the township form of government from 1862 until February 28, 1900. As a township, Fairmount and West Orange were governed by a committee consisting of five members, the office of chairman corresponding to that of mayor. Ambrose Condit was the first and only chairman. The first town clerk was Edmond Condit and the first tax collector, Lewis Condit. Simeon Harrison was the first chairman of the West Orange Township Committee.

The West Orange Police Department was established in 1884 and consisted of three patrolmen with William H. Bramford as captain and chief of police. The department had its headquarters in the Hedges Block at the time it was destroyed by fire. During the period the building was being rebuilt, the department was stationed in a small structure on the present site of the new municipal building. Chief Bramford retired in 1918 and Chief Patrick J. McDonough, who had been appointed to the department in 1900, was placed in charge.

As a result of the destruction of the Hedges Block in 1892, a fire department was organized by the township committee in 1894 with three paid men and eight on-call men. The new department was installed in a frame-constructed building on a lot at the corner of Whittingham Place and Valley Road. The plot was donated by Simeon H. Rollinson. He gave the town an option to purchase the land, which was later exercised by the township committee. The first piece of apparatus was a horse-drawn hose wagon pulled by a pair of black horses, and a fire alarm system was installed in 1894. The No. 2 firehouse on Washington Street was constructed of brick and was occupied in 1904. The present fire headquarters replaced the wooden firehouse in 1908, and the Fourth Ward No. 3 firehouse was erected in 1929. All department members received full salaries in 1918. The first piece of motor apparatus was put into service in 1911 and by 1915 the department was completely motorized. The first head of the fire department was Owen Kennedy, whose title was foreman. He held the office for less than a year and was succeeded by James J. Sheehan, who served as chief from 1894 until 1926. Chief Sheehan was succeeded by Martin T. Kennedy.

The residents of West Orange are well served by their local government, police, and fire departments. All three have acquired a splendid reputation for efficiency in performance and are the pride of the community.

This is a 1937 photograph of the old West Orange Town Hall, which was located on Northfield Road. During the time that this building was used as the town hall, West Orange was governed by a committee of five members. These members administered one of five town departments. Executive responsibility was divided, with each commissioner acting independently. These same commissioners formed the legislative body. The mayor, whose duties were mostly ceremonial, was one of the commissioners.

The new West Orange Town Hall was built in 1937 at Memorial Park, 66 Main Street. The residents of West Orange recognized the inherent weakness of commission government and voted in 1961 to adopt a new municipal charter—Mayor Council Plan B of the Optional Municipal Charter Law of New Jersey, known as the Faulkner Act. In 1980, the municipality's name was changed to the Township of West Orange.

West Orange's town council was launched on its four-year term in 1938. During the council's tenure, West Orange was governed under a commission form of government. The township is currently governed by a Mayor-Counsel form of government; a recent petition to revert to the commission administration was rejected during a 1997 election.

This is the old West Orange Post Office and Water Company building. The patrons in front of the office are waiting for letters to arrive, perhaps from as far away as the West Coast.

A West Orange police officer patrols the town center with an early K-9 unit in 1910. An interesting police dispatch occurred in the early 1920s when Frank Morris, a newspaper reporter for the *Newark News* and several New York City newspapers, received a call from a town resident that an "ungodly monster was peering into his window." Morris called the police department, which dispatched a vehicle to the area to look for a monster that was described as "red, with all kinds of shapes." Police on the scene discovered the "red monster" was a deer who had sauntered through a backyard clothesline and caught a pair of red flannel pajamas on his antlers. Morris, who witnessed the deer's capture, dubbed the incident, "The reappearance of the Jersey Devil in the Watchung Mountains."

The West Orange Police Department marches in a parade marking the town's bicentennial in 1978. One hundred years before this the town had no police force. In 1882, four thousand residents depended on the Orange Police Department for law enforcement and public safety. By 1884, however, the town launched an independent department, staffed by three patrolmen. In 1890, the department had grown to ten men. Two separate police headquarters were destroyed by fire before the department moved to its current home adjacent to the town hall.

This fire station located on the corner of Valley Road and Whittingham Place was built in 1907. This was the fire department's first brick headquarters. The first fire headquarters was located in a two-story wooden house adjacent to this structure. The Valley Road fire station was comprised of a three-man company and was responsible for fire control.